FLOWER FASHION
FANTASIES

MING-JU SUN

FLOWER ART
COLORING BOOK

DELUXE EDITION

4 BOOKS IN 1!

DOVER PUBLICATIONS, INC.
MINEOLA, NEW YORK

NOTE

From glamorous gowns made from vines, flower petals, and a variety of flora, to detailed table-top flower arrangements, to abstract designs based on flower patterns, this interesting collection of coloring pages showcases the many ways that flowers can be used in art. A unique opportunity for the experienced colorist, over 100 illustrations provide limitless possibilities for experimentation. Plus, perforated pages make displaying your work easy.

Bibliographical Note

Flower Art Coloring Book: Deluxe Edition is a new compilation of previously published Dover books by Ming-Ju Sun, Susan Bloomenstein, Charlene Tarbox, and Jessica Mazurkiewicz. See source information below.

Source Information

Floral Designs (2012), *Flower Fashion Fantasies* (2012), *Beautiful Flower Arrangements* (2013), *Fabulous Flowers* (2013).

International Standard Book Number

ISBN-13: 978-0-486-77932-4
ISBN-10: 0-486-77932-7

Manufactured in the United States by RR Donnelley
77932710   2015
www.doverpublications.com

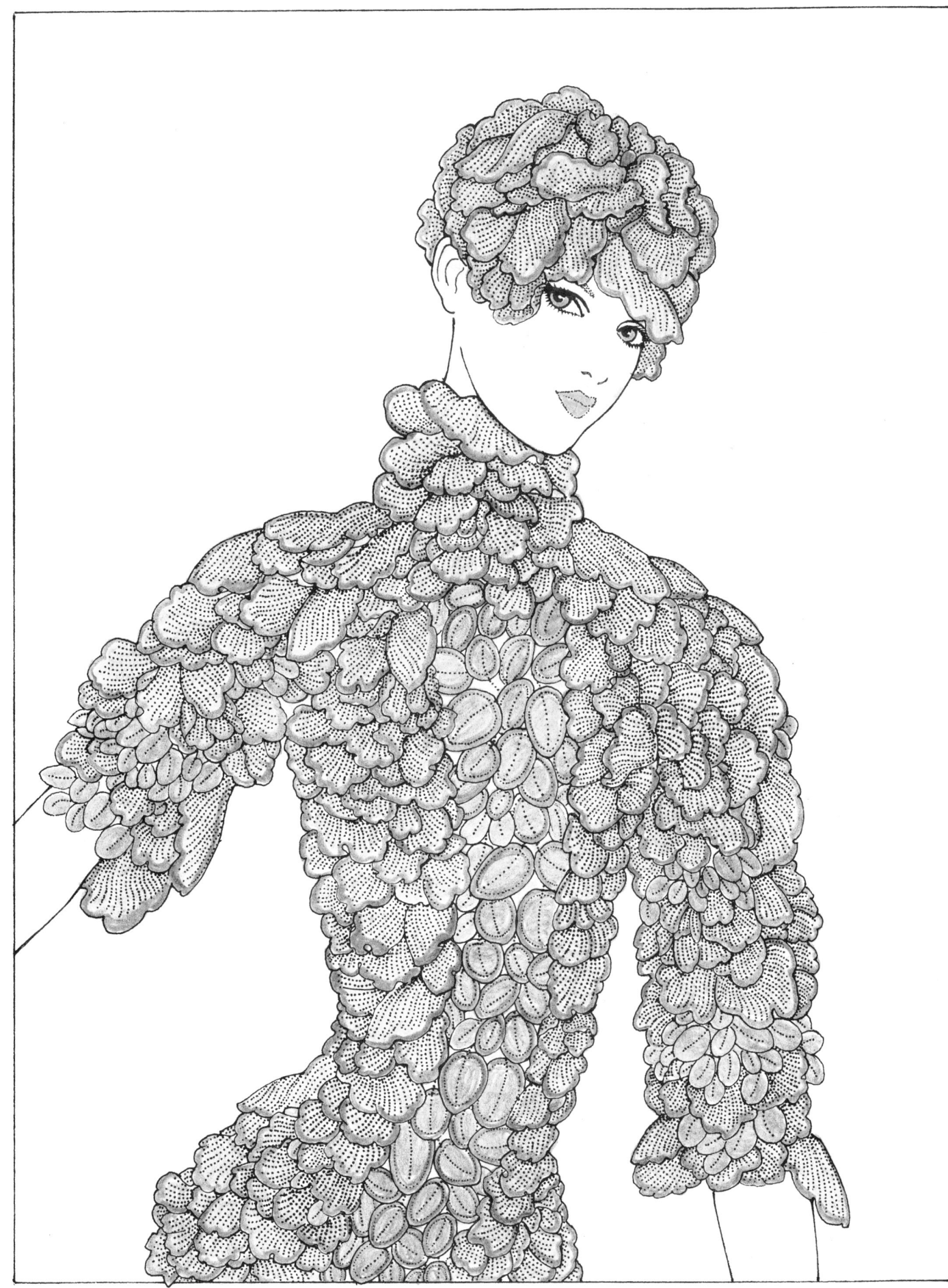

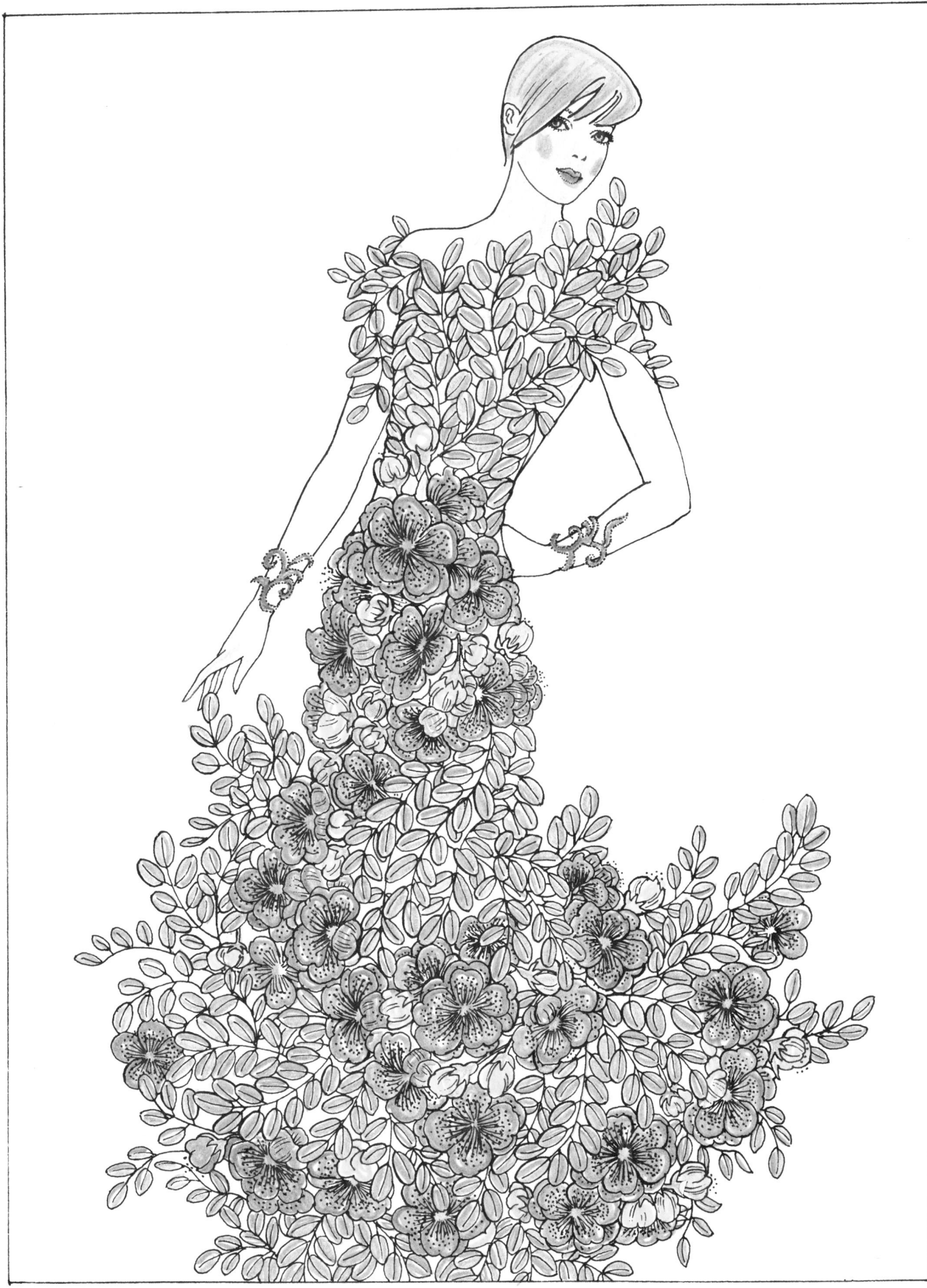

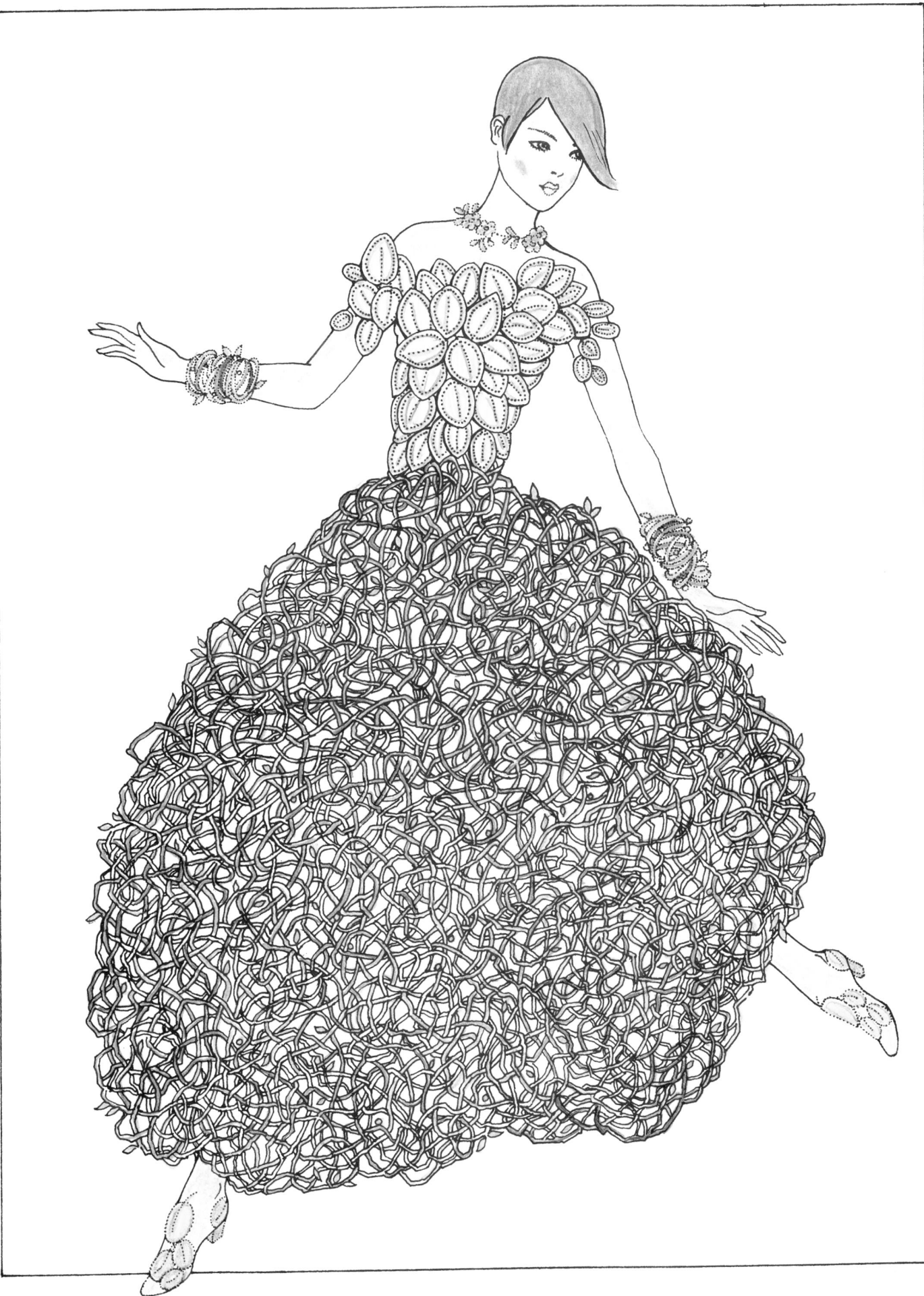

FABULOUS FLOWERS

SUSAN BLOOMENSTEIN

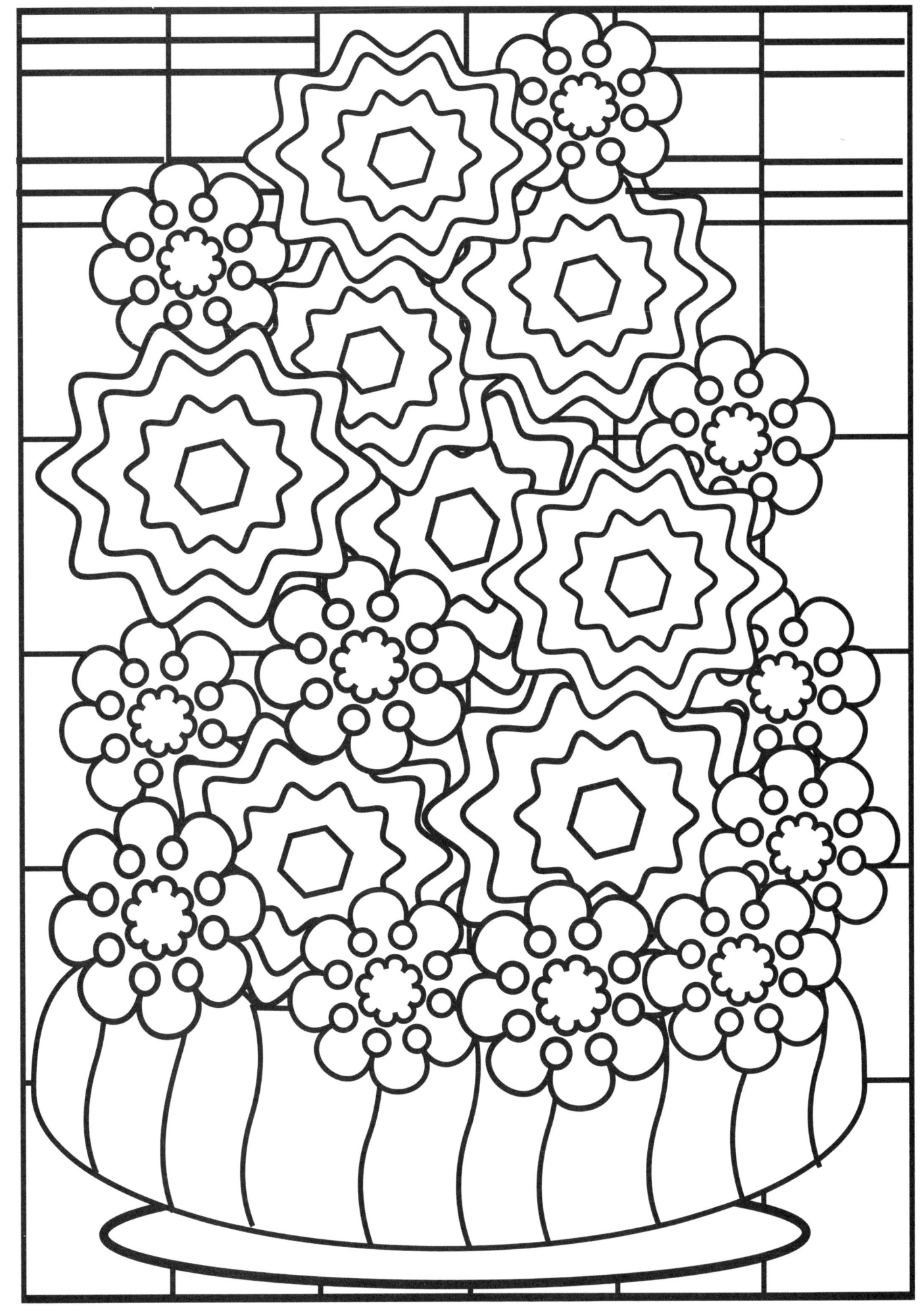

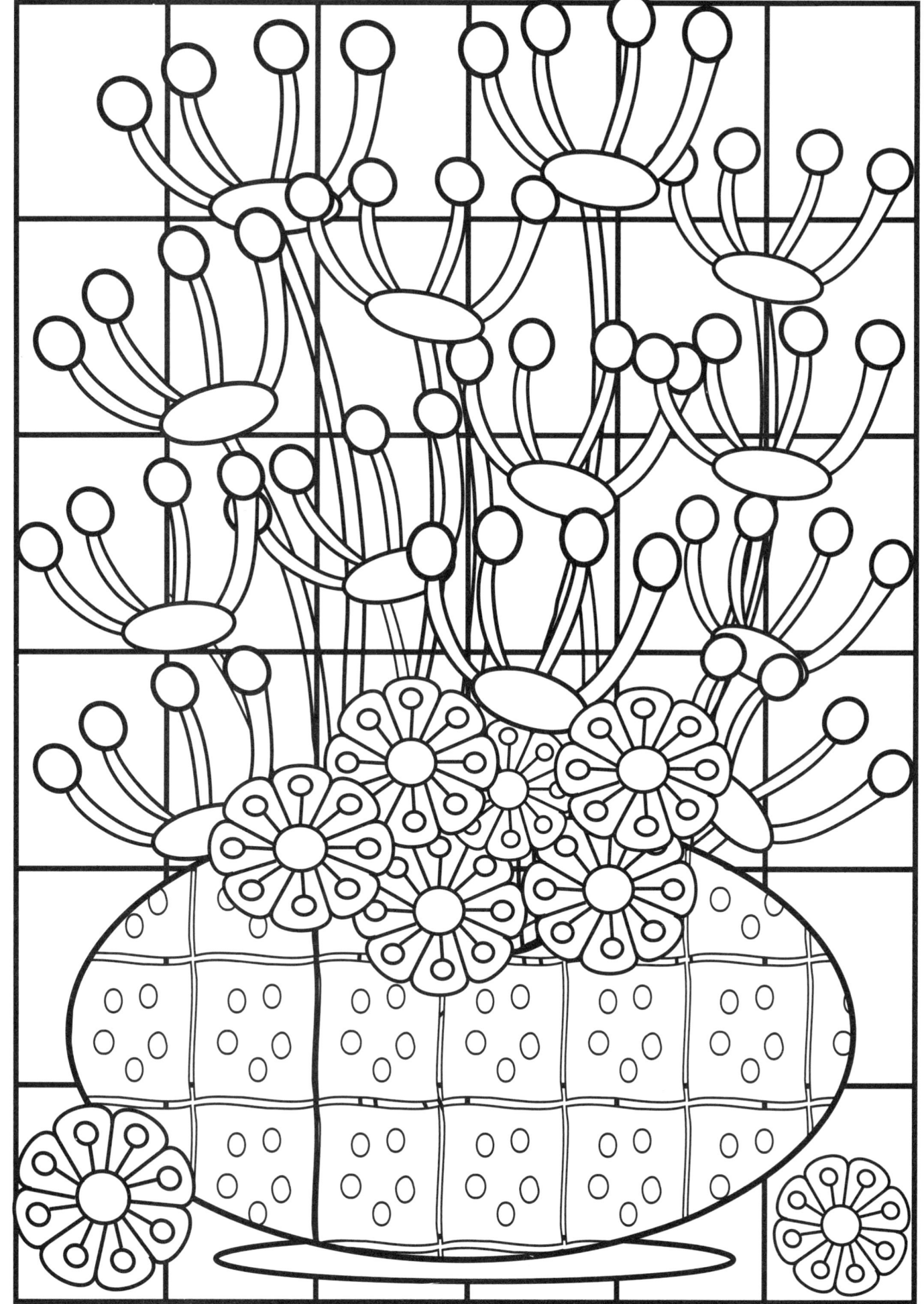

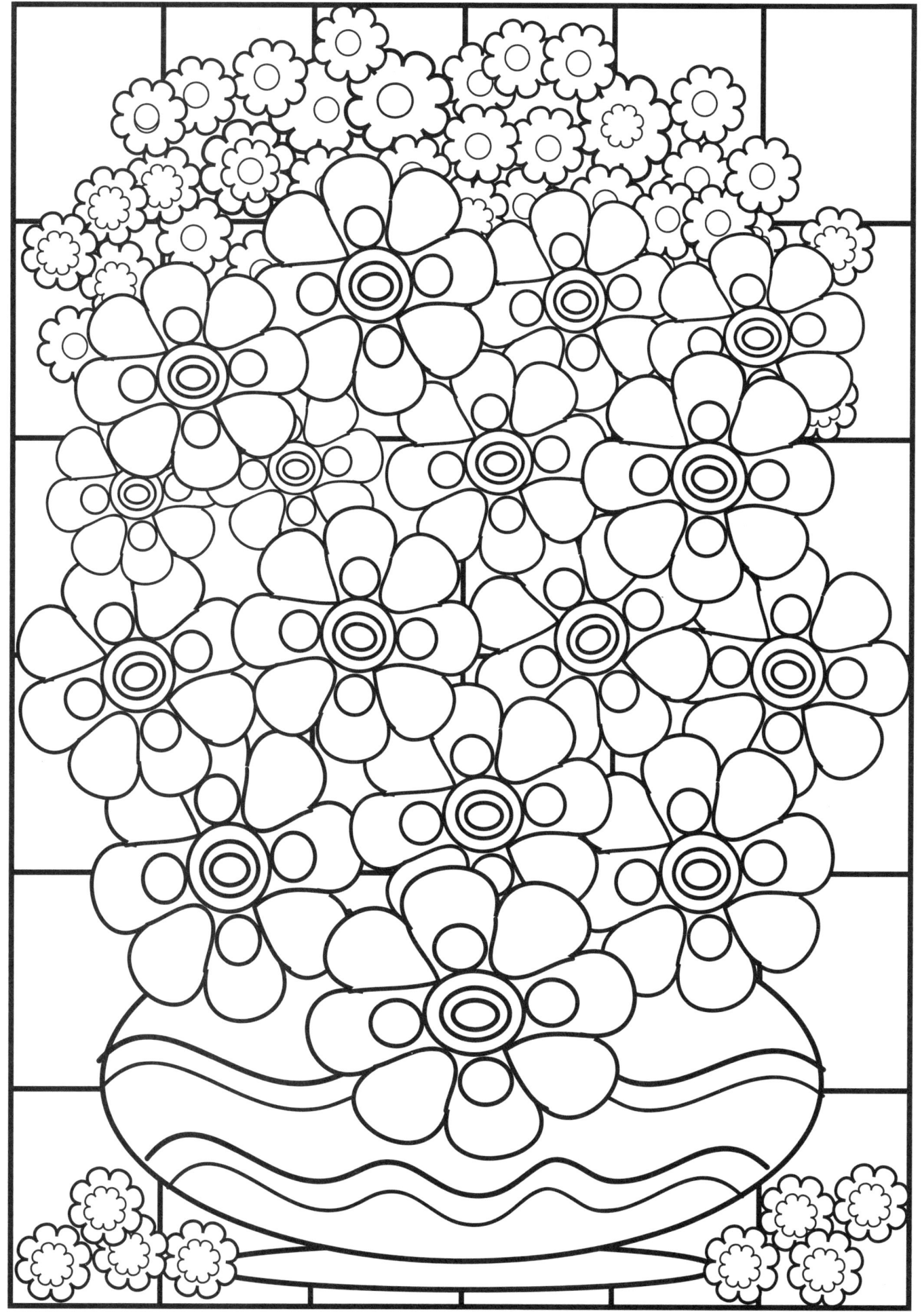

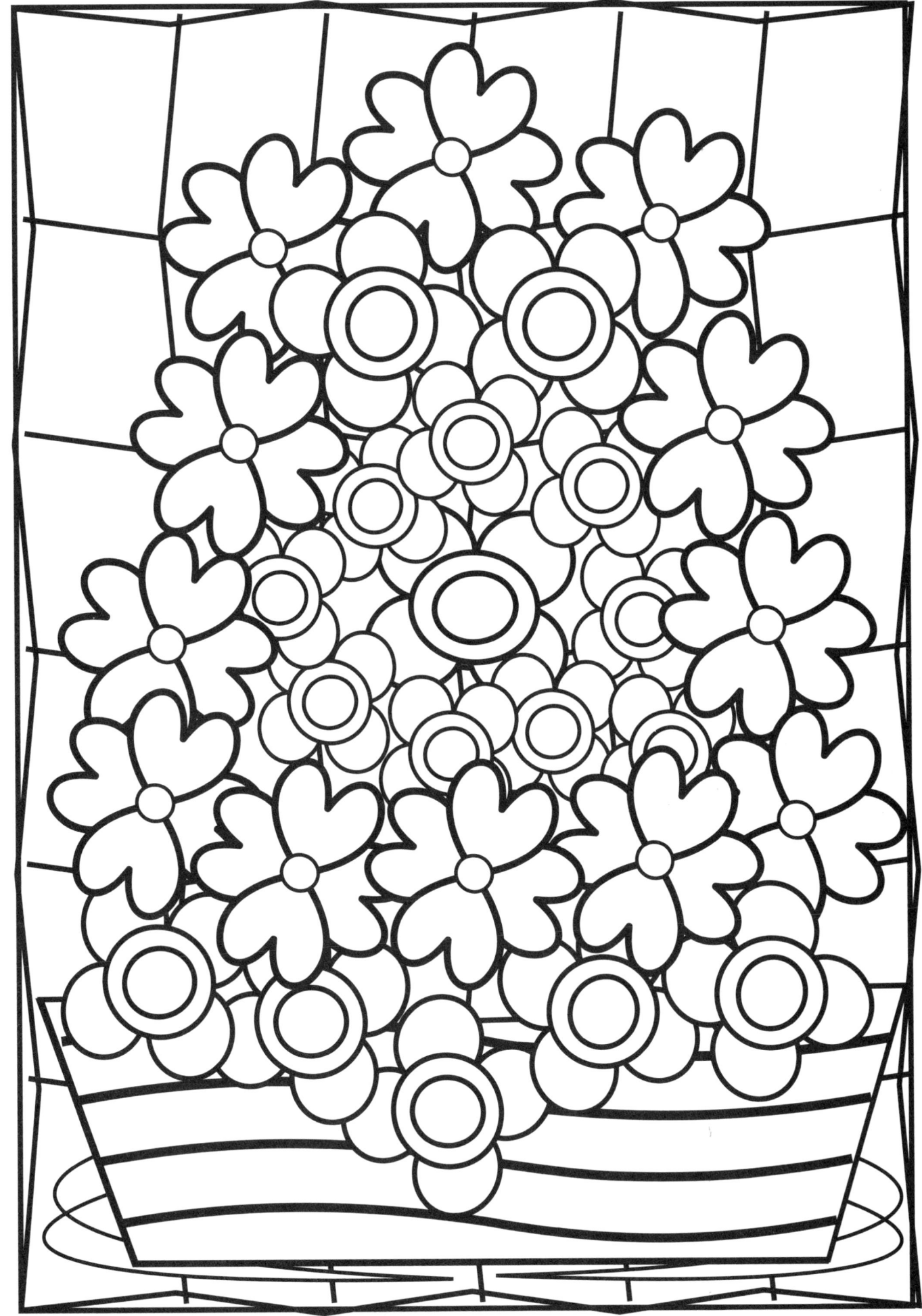

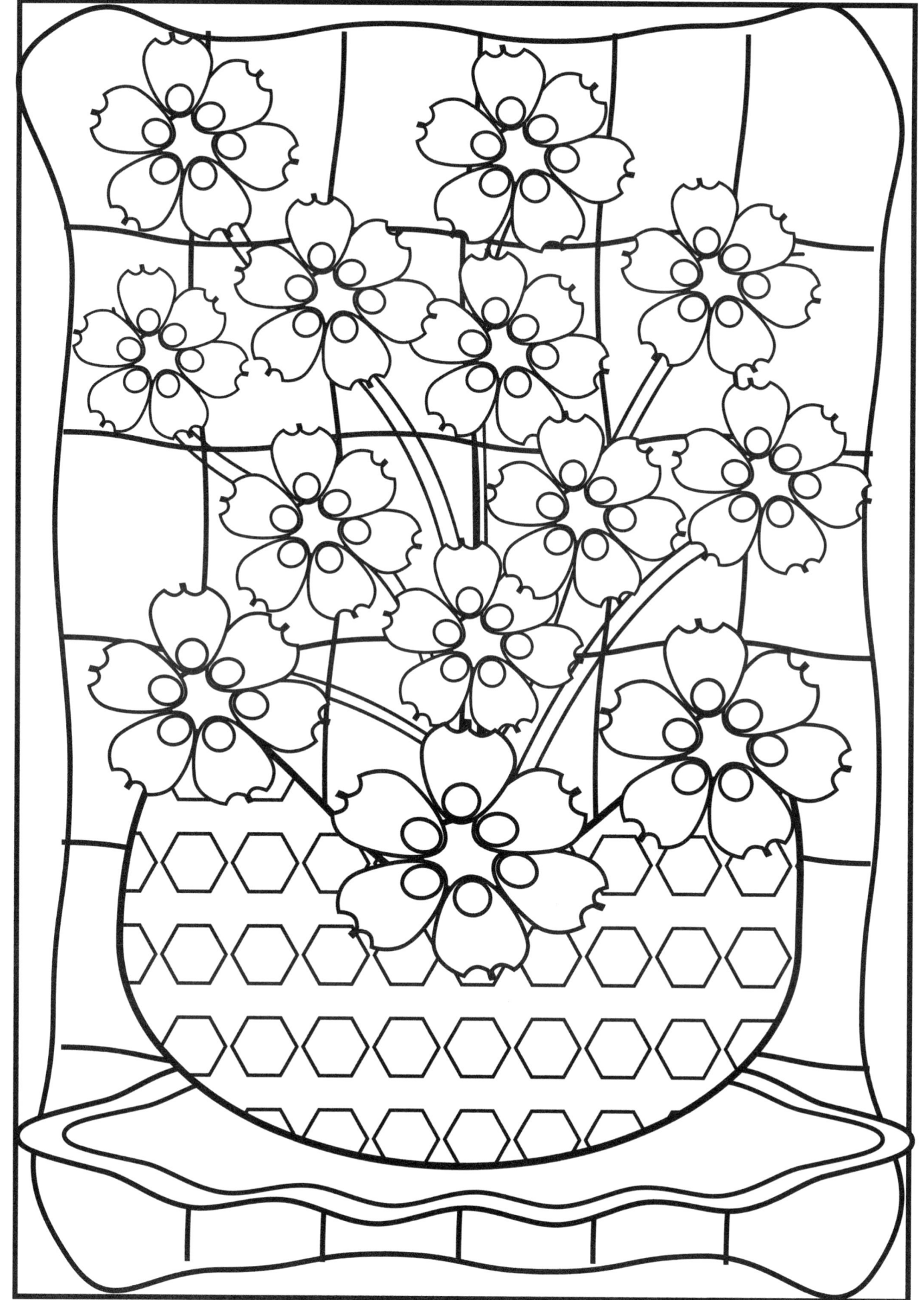

Beautiful Flower Arrangements

Charlene Tarbox

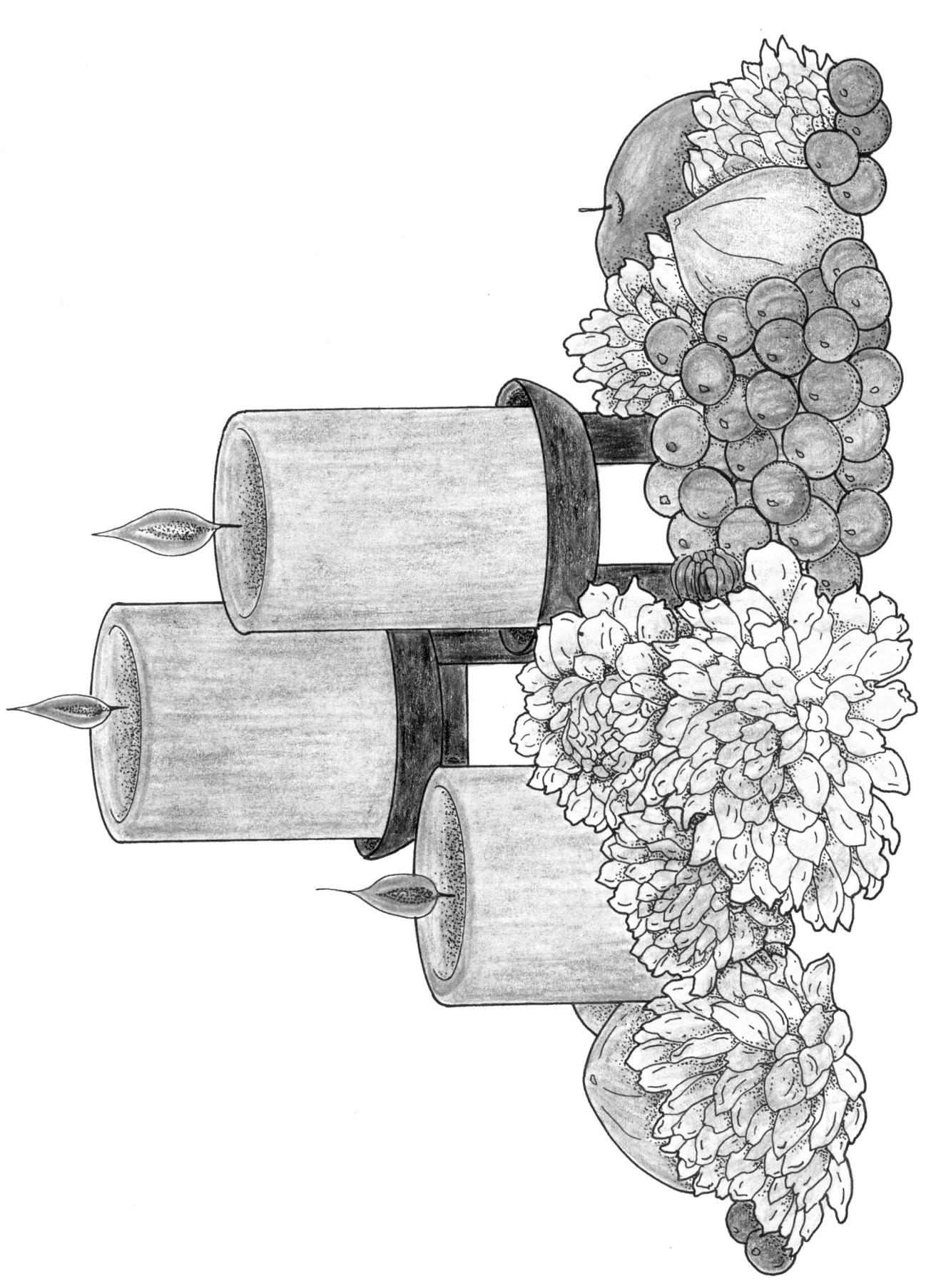

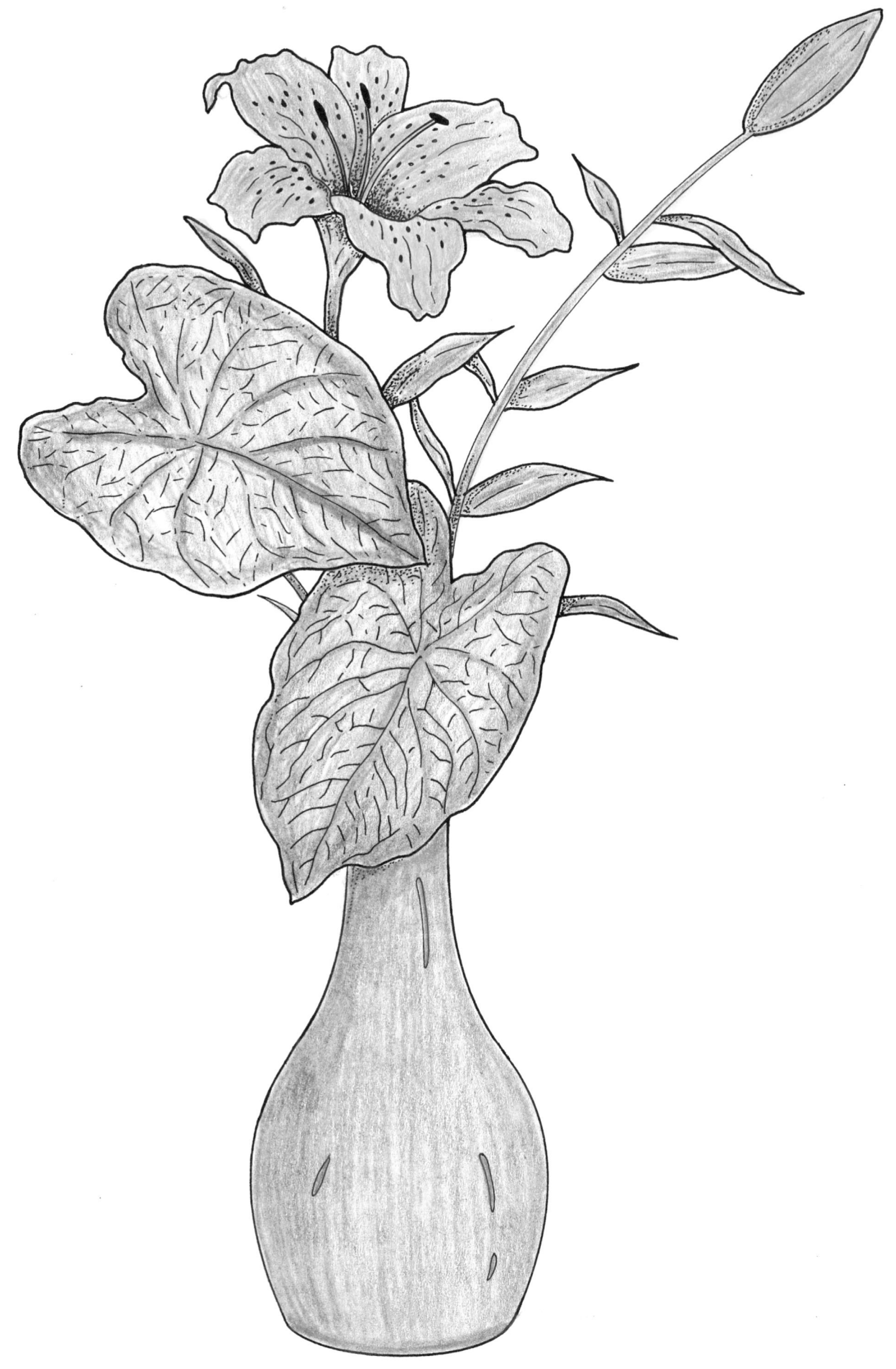

FLORAL
DESIGNS

JESSICA MAZURKIEWICZ